What Makes a Woman Beautiful

For Liam
In all this beauty
inner + outer.
Love —
Joan Logghe
2010

Joan Logghe

Pennywhistle Press
Santa Fe
1993

Poems from this collection have previously appeared in the following publications: *Noctiluca, Women's Review of Books, Hembra, Santa Fe Reporter, Puerto Del Sol, Visions International* and *Fish Drum.*

First edition
Printed in the United States of America
by Ortiz Printing Shop, Santa Fe

ISBN: 0-938631-15-2

For additional copies, address orders to: Harbinger House
P.O. Box 42948
Tucson, AZ 85733-2948
(602) 326-9595
FAX 326-8684

Note: Poems with the following mark: ∿
at the bottom of the page are continued on the next page.

Contents

Introduction

"What makes a woman beautiful?"

Joan Logghe poses the question with this sensual and hard-edged collection of new poems. What makes this question radical, even now, at the close of the second millennium, is that it is finally a woman who not only asks, but answers the question.

I can think of no better authority than Joan, whose poems lay open, like unbuttoned overcoats, revealing the raw and complicated beauty of the woman—the real woman inside the woman.

Poet of motherhood, sisterhood, daughterhood, and the "sweet watered-down" mayhem of marriage, Joan's poems trace the truly beautiful outline of the feminine where "sky meets body," and night-filled eyes know the "rainy faces of children." Like her archetypal character Sophia, Joan builds a shrine to *la mujer*, her language like "bits of broken colored glass" to catch our dawning awareness, her metaphors votive candles shining straight into the reader's eye.

These are poems hard to read lightly: like Josie Bliss' lips on Pablo Neruda's shoes, they are "warm right through the leather." Some are as white-knuckled as a clenched fist that opens, suddenly, to reveal the chiseled treasure inside—"the odor of rivers and Mother". . ."a bucket of roses (that) rise in your throat". . . "a full diamond walking hard toward a horizon."

Others are soft, sensually sprawled out like Frida "waiting for nothing" on white sheets "struck by lightning." Still others ring with the unadulterated rage of the female victim, the raped women of Bosnia, the indistinguishable "tears of a hundred women."

These are poems set on a Ceylonese boardwalk and on an icy stage on the road to Moscow. They sing, too, of a Sephardic night in Española, New Mexico, the strangely seductive and culturally complex community Joan and I share as our home. From the "Sonic North to the Sonic South," as Joan once wrote, stretches the dark body of this town named after an anonymous Spanish lady. Joan knows this elusive lady and her endless array of garments.

In the title poem, Joan quotes her mother, owner of the "Salon of Beauty", as saying: "Beauty's an emotion. It's a classic,/a well tailored garment that lasts."

In the tradition of Neruda, Joan weaves the everyday stuff of life—"two-for-one Cokes," "Oil of Olay," and the "one vine loaded with white grapes"—into shimmering garments of beauty. They are not one-size-fits-all, and that is the measure of their wisdom and, yes, their longevity. These poems are, above all, carefully tailored to the idiosyncrasies of the individual woman.

Jim Sagel
Española, New Mexico

To my mother, Beti Weitzner, who lives in beauty.

Who can refuse to live her own life?

—Anna Akhmatova
from *Way of All the Earth*

SUNSET DRAWS SOPHIA DOWN

It was the most beautiful spring,
the spring she couldn't decide
if she were happiest or saddest.

It was the spring she wanted to run off—
never see her children again
because she couldn't stand
that much love.

Her husband seemed to grow
up, then down, then sideways.
Nothing he did called her
in that old enticing way.

She had never seen such dimensions
in the clouds, layers so thick
she made time to admire them.

It was the season of morning walks
where the magpies and woodpeckers flew
and jackrabbits leapt out of her way.

Some days she woke up a teenager
others, a grandmother.
She struggled between passion and despair
sadness that comes down
straight from the ancestors.

It was the long spring. The fragrant one.
Her children stepped to the side
when she passed.
Her husband stopped touching her.
The phone never rang.

She lived alone inside the family.
But the flowers she planted
grew with a force not common to the desert.

SOPHIA BUILDS A SHRINE

During her middle years
when the children looked
all glowing and strong
like pups, like colts,
she and her husband stood
frayed and tattered
at the back of the photographs.
They looked older then
than at retirement.

She needed more
than frozen corn
and mended jeans,
a cure beyond dried herbs
manzanilla and aluzema.

She stole time from summer.
A thief of after work minutes
and the baby in bed
the two older ones
fighting over dishes.
Her husband stood smoking
on the porch
beside himself with sunset.

East of the house
quiet among piñons
she drew a crescent with her foot
so that the moon would fall
full face rising, on the Virgin.
The statue she bought to town,
called her in whispers, "Lupita."

~

On Sundays they picked rocks.
The kids ran the arroyos
tossed stones onto the pick-up bed
and rode home squabbling.
Sophia touched them each
then sent them in for lemonade,
sorted granite and limestone.

She domed the nicho
and in wet mortar stuck
bits of broken colored glass
in rays to catch the sun,
a corona of daylight.

Next spring she planted
a few beans at the base
some blue corn
each with a blessing.
And she went wild with flowers:
double petunias
crackerjack marigolds.

On dark nights
she said many prayers.
Wrote some on paper scraps
tucked under the rocks.
She'd bring sea shells, ribbons,
and milagros. Whatever pleased her,
she'd bring, and many votive candles
burned and shined.

People say
Sophia seems younger
since she built that shrine,
a rose, blooming out of season.

SOPHIA'S BREASTS

No matter his bitterness with life
her husband loved her breasts
hummed into them
he was forever
a lover or newborn.

And they were fresh
and her breasts were small
miracles of milk.
The third day after birth
they would engorge.
One infant cry
milk would let down
and drip onto her blouse.
She'd smile, pick the baby up
feel close to animals
the nanny goat, the ewe.
That was not all she felt.

Her breasts were always young
and from another time.
She and her husband
slept in the mountains.
She took off her shirt
and he grew faint
with the odor of rivers and Mother.

Her rosary was made of rose,
real petals, not scented wood,
and her fingers for years were sweet
with the fragrance of death.
Two children in four years
there was a lifting and falling
a sighing then.

~

Years had a way of stacking up:
firewood, dried apricots and pears.
Time compressed, her body changed
but not her breasts.
She likes to sun them
bare in the face of God.
Her face is fragile paper now.
Her breasts are from another time.

SOPHIA WRITES HER FRIEND
WHO HAS MOVED

I could tell you of town,
trucks loaded with melon
a dollar a basket
and the sky that color, melon,
after a dinner of garden corn.

I could tell you my husband
remembered my birthday
and our anniversary.
He's really trying hard.
The children are happy at school
and stopped that fighting, remember?

I could tell you we have had
plenty of rain and that summer
was cooler than usual.
I saw Vicente at Farmer's Market
and he's much better.

~

Instead I write you
that my truck got stuck in the arroyo.
A flash flood came out of nowhere.
Hail got the tomatoes.
I tell you he spanked my son
a bit too hard, and that they
won't help with the chores.

My eyes are fixed on the weeds
not the pumpkins hiding inside them
or the volunteer tomatoes
and one vine loaded with white grapes.

I tell you who died
and one close call.
No one dances at the weddings
like you used to.

We are emptier and wine
is not as full of laughter,
for sure, we miss you.
How is your son, your car?
Have you gotten a better job?
Who do you know there?

SOMETHING

Sophia had a secret even Sophia
didn't know. Something about
candles at night, no taste of pork
in her grandmother's house. Something.

A shadowed memory of her grandmother
in her dark bedroom, her voice nearly
a whisper, "It passes down through the women. "
That and "Tell your daughter. "

Something about the farolitos lined up,
a top to spin. "Our family came from Spain,
not Mexico, hundreds of years ago. This
is your great-grandfather, Israel.

See how handsome he was." Sophia recalls it all
but mixed with other conversations, the smell
of pine at Christmas, candles at mass,
the sight of blood at butchering each fall.

Something about candles to Saint Esther.
It didn't make sense. "We came here from Spain.
Look hard at this photograph." Her mother's voice
in the kitchen light, flour in the air.

She'll tell her daughters something soon.
She's been meaning to. For hundreds of years.
She'll tell them soon. She will.

MARRIAGE

Sometimes in the evening,
in the hot evening, sometimes Sophia
and Manny drive into town.
They park at the Sonic Drive-in
facing north. There's a green lawn
and some elms across the way.

We can pretend, she says,
that we're in the mountains.
It's cool here. The roof
is full of birds, I can hear them
but I can't see what kind.

They get two-for-one Cokes
and sit together in the truck, close.
Sophia takes Manny's hand,
he's not the type in public.
It's just summer. Sophia
takes ice and rubs some on her face.

They don't have another thing to say.
There's traffic, the birds,
the slurping of soft drinks.
Marriage, the sweet watered down.

SOPHIA'S GONE

Death came not by spider
as she'd always feared. Not
by snake, not by fire. Death
did not come in a fanfare of pain
as in an auto wreck, she'd clutched
the pick-up seat so many years.

Death did not come playing an old
guitar and singing serenades.
Death was not wearing silver,
but sweetly in the afternoon, long light
slanted through geranium, the shadow
on the wall, scent of iris in her mouth.

Death at last, alone as she was,
"Welcome, welcome, death." It was enough
to live this life this long.
She placed a picture of the two of them
she and Manny, an anniversary
right on her heart and she let go.

She thought her children would be near
but death had other plans, called heart,
heart, sweet selfless heart. He grabbed
her much too hard. Her right arm waving
everything goodbye. Sophia's done.
She's gone. Her brain a final shot of song.
Her hair growing right to the end.
White, white veils, Sophia is bride again.

A FRIDA KAHLO/DIEGO RIVERA NIGHT

Last night you woke me, Diego Rivera
on TV. Wrapped me in blankets, fed me
tea. At last I was cared for the way
an artist ought to live. Catered to,
my vision understood in primacy.

Women need a love like this. I look past you
to their love crimes. How impossible they were
to one another. What fuel. Frida in color
footage in New York, Rockefeller Center.
Voice over says he had three loves: painting,

Frida, and women. My eyes on a Mexican full moon.
Making love, my breasts become Diego Rivera's eyes.
As he grew old, they fell from his head
from so much looking. I see the world this way,
led by my breasts to love. Smell with my heart.

FRIDA'S SUMMER

There's a pitcher of water in the sun, it fills with dust
even as I drink. A storm's blowing.

The paint thickens and dries. A little girl ran
up to me, held out a flower. No! It was actually a bone.

White, white. Examine the dog at my feet. His teeth
persuade me. The full moon of August is the loudest.

All the August moons of my life line up. You caught me
with my hair down, that's only for catastrophe.   ~

Thunder was my lover. Calamity and every four years
the grave turned over under the eyes in the courtyard.

I lay my head under the grass of Diego's waist.
All the buses of the world are coming for me.

Diego has a bite of cool melon for an excuse.
He always had plenty.

Pass me that avocado. Excuses are worthless.
It's your life I want to bite. Throw the pit over here.

Let's paint my face from another angle. From chin to hair.
Or show only the back of my head, I can't face the front again.

I am waiting for nothing. Everything waits for me.
Here, clean this brush, *por favor*.

Death would be better. Bitter. Water
makes the wounds sound sweet.

Excesses all of them. Leave me alone!
You are about to break ground, he said.

My painting or my life, I asked. Women gather in
sheets struck by lightning. This is unlucky.

A woman at the end of the century will replace
her face with mine. Museum. Mausoleum.

You startled me. I thought I was beyond
surprise. I'm as much a woman as you are.

I don't expect to sleep at night.
I've made a profession of insomnia.

BURNING THE PAPERS

Memory has been unbelievably keen. The past
crowds me and demands something. What?
— Anna Akhmatova
The Fear and the Muse,
The Story of Anna Akhmatova

They smoked alone in a room in Leningrad.
She was out of favor, not allowed to write.
On thin paper for cigarettes, she wrote her poem down.
Memory is a carrier pigeon. Memory is infectious disease.

They spoke with looks, and Russia, that land
of too many eyes, looked on. Moscow, city
of too many ears, eavesdropped. Words were the fish
her friend ate with her eyes. Landlocked in a city

of iron gates. A repository for "Requiem."
They set fire to the papers. Every night a lit match.
This is what memory was made for, not things past
but things pressing. Urgency, bad politics.

She took the same route home to quatrains
in her feet. Became archival, times remarkable.
Pain memorized the last time I sat famously alone.
I too have words to burn and I know grief.

Nobody's pain can hold a candle to another's.
My friend says, "I want you to be happy." The papers
whisper as they curl, "That's not what you were made for."
My heart is a two party system that doesn't work.

JOSIE BLISS

> *I went so deep into the soul and life of these*
> *people that I lost my heart to a native*
> *woman. In the street she dressed like an*
> *Englishwoman and used the name Josie*
> *Bliss, but in the privacy of her home, which*
> *I soon shared, she shed those clothes and*
> *that name to wear her dazzling sarong and*
> *her secret Burmese name.*
>
> —*Memoirs*, Pablo Neruda

I.

Dressed in her grey suit of English cut
she couldn't hide those eyes.

In the room she removed her shoes, mine.
She rubbed my soles with thin hands.

Oh, I had been to the Snake Temple of Penang
where candelabras coil with coral snakes

and the dank walls house a thousand serpents.
Lethal or not, the shadows that move turn snake,

are indeed forms of God called snake,
the Russel's viper, python, fer-de-lance.

All laze and drowse, sated by eggs and milk
set out in bowls in the temple dark.

It's silent there, the walls seem eaten.
It was this terror and languor both

I felt set out in the hands
of Josie Bliss.

She had another name that I won't tell,
her Burmese name locked to her.

~

She took me on, dark marvel, who fell first?
We fell together into our locked temple.

And she stayed on top of me all night,
my breath was forced, the in, the out.

She, in her snake eye, she with frangipani
on her perfumed feet, the incense of the Snake Temple.

Burmese, you ask? English? Josie Bliss
came from solitude and landed on earth with two bare feet.

She lived her life horizontally, on edge.
I say, tigress, lioness, panther.

She stretched out. I welcomed her
and she staked her claim and stayed.

II.   *Facing you*
                I am not jealous.

                Come with a man
                at your back,
                come with a hundred men in your hair,
                come with a thousand men between
                        your bosom and your feet ...

                "Always," The Captain's Verses, Pablo Neruda

I couldn't write. For weeks
we lazed all morning,
went out at noon
when it was already too hot.

We walked to the cafe.
We acted there a normal life.
In her rooms which I came to share
nothing was further from true.   ~

She was clad in teeth.
At night she wore only jealous teeth.
She wrestled the poems out,
they took too much from her.

She stole the poems out of my skin
with a voice that sounded like the sea,
sometimes murmur, also undertow.
There was a shipwreck lurking there.

I was a simple man who simply loved.
She was cut from day and cut from night.
She was a dazzling fabric of flowers,
this was the Josie Bliss I came for.

I'd wake at night. There she stood,
a knife above my heart,
"This for the loves you've had before,
this for the ones to come."

Everything in color was a threat,
the hips of women, birds, leaves of a tree.
Anything I loved that served my soul
she wanted to cut out.

I would have stayed with her until I died.
I would have made her a poem of love.
As it was, I stole myself away at night,
abandoned all I owned, my books, my clothes.

I got another consul job, sailed for Ceylon
and there I stayed. I took a servant boy,
a mongoose for a pet. These served me
to forget the nights with Josie Bliss.

Though I am a poet of love, never
has there been the words for this.
The middle of the night, waking to a knife
of love, to cut the poems out.

~

III.

In Ceylon life went along. I wrote
once more, dined out. My mongoose
charmed the neighbors, who laughed
as it fled the cobra it was meant to fight.
I had the solitude I craved and hated, both.

One afternoon, came Josie Bliss again
in her sarong, with a woven sleeping mat,
a rice sack on her back, as if
there were no rice field in Ceylon.
In out of the brightest time of day.

She had jazz records we both loved at her breast.
I said she'd have to go, but she refused,
camped by my door, began to cook, insult
my servant. Everyone who called had her
to pass. She chased a girl who'd come to tea.

She railed she'd burn my house down and she would.
I pleaded with my love, my terrorist.
It was talking to a gale, reasoning
with natural disaster. My neighbors
called the police, she'd have to leave Ceylon.

I booked her ticket home, stroked once her hair,
dusty and unkempt, the beauty gone. She
was wailing as I walked her to the boat.
On the boardwalk her wild eye caught mine,
she howled a monkey's howl and grabbed my feet.

She kissed the shoes. I felt her lips, warm
right through the leather. And when she rose
her face was white with the polish of my shoes
and streaked with tears. I didn't kiss her
or I'd kiss the gist of love. I sent her home.

MARIE TAGLIONI

from the legend inscribed in Joseph Cornell's box,
The Jewel Casket of Marie Taglioni

Then it came. The horse beat, the heart's horse
coming. Cantering blood, illuminated bone.
The carriage tottered, like children pretending
to be drunk. I stood the road, shouted, "Stop!"
I wore my panther skin, the sword of a highwayman.

At the carriage door, I spoke, blowing the snow
off my moustache. "Excuse this intrusion. I promise
you no harm." Sleepy of face and pale, Marie Taglioni,
poised between fear and imperial disgust. "Take
my jewels, what few I own. They're yours."

"No, no, no, I'm here only to see you dance,
I must." The snow fell like small fans. A moment
of feathers, an instant of sea foam as she stepped
down. Part of her understood, said "Driver, my case."
I spread the stage of panther skin, held still.

The driver moved in trance, the quiet snow
fell long. She tied the ribbons on her shoes,
looked up, a girl trying out for the Corps de Ballet.
The shoes. The shoes. On a thin stage she went
on toe and danced for me, an audience of one.

No music, but horses. No light, but ice. Alive
on the Moscow Road. Off came her travel coat.
The color of her dress I couldn't tell. Her waist
like a sigh. Leaping, she turned to snow, she spun
my breath. Turning me into a man, turning her

~

into herself, perfectly so. I said, "Brava,"
and clapped. I deeply bowed, so low a bow
I felt faint, like a woman inside me swooned.
I kissed her hand, her hem, and dared her face,
vivid with what light the snow allowed.

Legends grow legends. They say she never forgot.
I've heard she takes a piece of ice, places
it among diamonds in her box of jewels,
watches it melt on the dressing table,
and dances.

WAR CRIMES

dedicated to the women of Bosnia

The red ribbon used to tie the gift, and then
the child's hair, ravels. Becomes a gag.
Becomes the knot of infinity, a thing to hold
in your hand as you leave your body as spoils.

Your body becomes a piñata, a birthday vessel.
Men are hitting it blindfolded with a stick
only you are the one who can't see, and instead
of wrapped candies and treats, out spills your hair,

your breasts, eyes, shoes, and your purse full of coins
is now full of strange seed and your gifts fall
into all the hands at once. You didn't want to share,
not this. A thing once known as pain crosses over

from feeling into shock. And a slap of light unhinges
what is left of a moon. And silent. Torn scarf,
rapid water, and a rip tide, all in body. Dense salt,
a bucket of roses rises in your throat

~

and you start a long scream. If the Bosnian women sang,
a red ribbon would rise out of their mouths and
find its way around the neck of the men, unsacred,
whose fingers smell of iron, breath, brute as poison.

Nobody wants to dwell in the basement of torture,
lift their skirt to try and find the soprano. Screams
are not opera. Screams tumble out of cave mouths, wind
is their relative, a natural force like tornado.

When I gave birth, the best part was being kin
to all women who opened their legs and thighs, pushed
out a head and loved it. Every human I met became my son.
Every face fell back into newborn. When ravished

what can you do but rise? No further place to fall, your own
discovery of gravity. If the women were given back
their clothes and threads for mending, would they sew
the fingers of rapists to their cocks? Lips to hats?

Attack is a pattern of chaos and rapid fire
ugly. Homilies read like the whistles of wolves.
Or would they mend? Add extra embroidery, the stitch
called compassion stitch, French knots, red and blue roses.

I write from my comfort, an offer to carry something
holy and heavy. You show me your blue plate, the only
artifact left of your home. We strain into each other,
our bodies insulated with fiberglass batt of distance.

I have no sister. Call you sister, hand you a ribbon.
Tie back your beautiful, profaned hair, a Guernica
of pain on your face, a hosanna of hope. If words have power,
suck articulation back inside. After war, words must suffice.

THEORY OF TEARS

Tears come from tombs.
They condense on the granite tombstones of Vermont
and hitch rides west on the faces of women.

The tears of men come from the sides of skyscrapers
and the faces of shovels left out overnight.
Tears are more related to dew than to rain,

more to oceans than to lakes, and of oceans,
they are more related to the Pacific than the Indian
or Arctic, because of all the memories the Pacific stirs.

If you tasted the tears of a hundred women, you
could not tell them apart. They'd have a childbed
taste and a whiff of soup in the bouquet.

But men's tears, because there are so few shed
are so concentrated, so individual. You can taste
a desk in one and a tractor in another. One tastes

of mother and the other has no taste, because he has saved
all his tears for a million million years, like a God
of tears, a full diamond walking hard toward a horizon.

HIGH SCHOOL GRADUATION PANTOUM

The dark boy leans against his pick-up truck.
His heart widened into Romeo since he met my daughter.
I say to myself, "It's not worth creating a tragedy."
With the Blood Mountains behind them for Verona.

His heart widened into Romeo when he met my daughter,
a girl pulling him by the arms down the driveway
with the Blood Mountains behind them for Verona,
the wild plum blooming, they will make sour fruit.

A girl pulling him by the arms down the driveway,
not long ago, her arms reached, her face ached red for me.
The wild plum blooming, it will make sour fruit.
Passions so sweet, grape couldn't turn wine without it.

Not long ago her arms reached, her face ached red for me,
crying through play-pen bars as I gardened,
passion so sweet, grape couldn't turn wine without it.
I thinned lettuce, her stomach full of milk and need.

Crying through play-pen bars as I garden.
Time is a rascal magpie pecking at the corn.
I thinned lettuce, her stomach full of absence.
I sat next to her driving, yelling, "Brakes!"

Time is a rascal magpie, exotic in the corn.
A yogi asked, "What if this baby should die?"
I sit next to her driving, yelling, "Brakes!"
My heart beats audibly past midnight curfew.

A yogi asked, "What if this baby should die?
Her tongue is long." He wrote on his slate at Lama Mountain.
My heart beats audibly past midnight curfew.
At Christ in the Desert I cried in the chapel for loss.

Her tongue is long, he wrote on his slate in silence.
She's kissed a boy she loved and some she didn't.
At Christ in the Desert I cried in the chapel for loss.
I sat with older mothers who had moved on.

She's kissed a boy she loved and some she didn't.
The dark boy leans against his pick-up truck.
I sit with older mothers who had moved on.
I say to myself, "Let go. It's not worth creating a tragedy."

BEAUTY SALON SESTINA

My father met my mother at the dance.
She pressed her face against Semitic skin,
hers, powdered above a base of Oil of Olay.
"Yellow Bird" was her favorite song.
The floor slick as if waxed by soap.
His evening stubble catches her blond hair.

"I won't go gray. He likes my hair
the way he found me, a blond at a dance.
I liked him right away, tall, solid, smelling of soap.
I watched the way his collar touched his skin.
We'd dance and he'd be counting out the song,
'Fascinatin Rhythm.' By now I used Oil of Olay.

I'm not so young, my son is six. Oil of Olay
protects me from Pittsburgh. My profession is hair,
I know its ins and outs, its curl and song.
I run my beauty shop in six inch heels, dance
down corridors, my partners, vanity and skin.
I may expand, away from the scent of shaving soap.

Not that I don't love barber shops and men in soap,
my sweet husband's face lathered. Oil of Olay
needs a room of her own. I move to a hotel, where skin
is on holiday, an elevator ride, hair's
respite from the world. My specialty is color. Dance
right into my door and I'll sing you beauty's song.

'Yellow Bird,' I tell you that's a blond song.
Soon we'll be coloring and cutting, soaking fingers in soap
and water for manicure. Note that word 'cure' and dance
over to the dryer, read about Oil of Olay
from stacks of Vogue, fantasies of hair,
and barely bare lingerie, feel the lace on warm skin.

All the while, Harry is nearby. His skin
next to his shirt two blocks from me. My song
is 'I'm Just Wild About Harry,' I fix my hair
before leaving at six. Use a curl of manicure soap
to wash off the smell of perms. Oil of Olay
and I'm in the lobby, through revolving doors I dance

like Ginger Rogers is in my skin. No soap
opera, we're Broadway songs, we're rich as Oil of Olay.
Harry, in salt and pepper hair, my Fred Astaire. We dance."

A GIANT BEAUTY

The daughter becomes a woman. I'm mourning
the cut ribbons announcing the launch of the ship.
I spend her like a golden egg at market, take
home the basket, empty, singing.

I plant the magic beans and grow a giant beauty.
And then, with my masculine hands, I must chop
the vine, and grow inside myself the Tree of Life.
Sending the children off, the commerce of this story.

Back to the basic blessings. Bread, a few grapes,
the color of eggplant in the clouds. My heart
crackles like cellophane. Space. Space. I write her
free. Hand her her Gretel papers. Send her

by moonlight and on horseback. Send her to ovens
and to sweetness, to distances and wiles.
My daughter becomes a woman in a painting
on someone else's wall.

WHAT MAKES A WOMAN BEAUTIFUL

A face is only beautiful if pain knows it,
if eyes know night and the rainy faces of children.
If sky meets body, a woman is beautiful if stars.

I know a woman hunched over
who is lovely in the ways of herbs and healing.
I know a woman in a wheelchair with curled hands
who is elegant in the art of batik.
I know a woman who looks small against her orchard
and is so striking in the way of aging.

I know a woman who took on two children
and her life fills with the beauty trails of noise.
I know a woman who runs rapids. Her mouth
splits open laughing, an absurd river.
I know a woman who had many abortions
and her beauty is in a way of absence.
I know a woman who gave up drugs,
her life is an authentic clean bell.

I know a woman who drinks, her face
in the mirror a stark majesty of habit.
I know a woman who has no children, grows
flowers and writes, "I am not barren."
I know a woman who carries drinks on trays.
I know a woman who adores opera,
her mind splendid as an aria.

I know a woman who keeps horses,
her boots are shiny, her nails a fright.
I know a woman who sells real estate,
an enchantress of walk-in closets and Jacuzzis.
I know a woman who lights up if you fight her.
I know all manner of women, the radiant,
the alluring, the divine. And I know
the hideous flip-side, doubt .

~

My mother who owned the Salon of Beauty
should be consulted, face like a heart.
She would offer her expert opinion.
"To have yourself," she would say smiling.
It was her business, beauty. She'd say,
"Beauty's an emotion. It's a classic,
a well-tailored garment that lasts."

To Order These Other Titles in the **Pennywhistle** Chapbook Series, Contact:

PENNYWHISTLE PRESS
P.O. BOX 734
TESUQUE, NEW MEXICO, 87574
Telephone: (505) 982-2622
Fax Orders: (505) 982-6858

What Makes A Woman Beautiful by Joan Logghe
Introduction by Jim Sagel, ISBN 0-938631-15-2 $6.00

Decoy's Desire by Kerry Shawn Keys
Introduction by Gerald Stern, ISBN 0-938631-14-4 $6.00

Where You've Seen Her by Grace Bauer
Introduction by Robin Becker, ISBN 0-938631-11-X $6.00

Still the Sirens by Dennis Brutus
Introduction by Lamont B. Steptoe, ISBN 0-938631-09-8 $6.00

Portal by Joyce Jenkins
Introduction by Carolyn Kizer, ISBN 0-938631-18-7 $6.00

No Golden Gate for Us by Francisco X. Alarcón
Introduction by Juan Felipe Herrera, ISBN 0-938631-16-0 $6.00

Tesuque Poems by Victor di Suvero
Introduction by Pierre Delattre, ISBN 0-938631-17-9 $6.00

Further Sightings & Conversations by Jerome Rothenberg
Introduction by Michael Palmer, ISBN 0-938631-09-9 $5.00

Who is Alice? by Phyllis Stowell
Introduction by Sandra Gilbert, ISBN 0-938631-04-7 $5.00

The Sum Complexities of the Humble Field by Viola Weinberg
Introduction by Mary Mackey, ISBN 0-938631-06-3 $5.00

Sublunary by Jorge H.-Aigla
Introduction by Charles G. Bell, ISBN 0-938631-07-1 $5.00

The Width of a Vibrato by Edith A. Jenkins
Introduction by Robert Gluck, ISBN 0-938631-10-1 $5.00

The Fields by Richard Silberg
Introduction by Joyce Jenkins, ISBN 0-938631-05-5 $5.00

Full Turn by Sarah Blake
Introduction by Dorianne Laux, ISBN 0-938631-08-X $5.00

Hardwired for Love by Judyth Hill
Introduction by Miriam Sagan, ISBN 0-938631-13-6 $5.00

Falling Short of Heaven by Suzanne Lummis
Introduction by Austin Strauss, ISBN 0-938631-12-8 $5.00